DANIEL:
A LIFE TRANSFORMED
LISA CULVERWELL

Title   Daniel: A Life Transformed
Author   Lisa Culverwell

Copyright: Lisa Culverwell,
September, 2018

Published By Parables
       September, 2018

All Rights Reserved. No part of this book may be reproduced or utilized in any form or by any means, electronic or mechanical, including photocopying, recording, or by any information storage and retrieval system, without permission in writing from the author.

Unless otherwise specified Scripture quotations are taken from the authorized version of the New King James Bible.

ISBN 978-1-945698-71-2
Printed in the United States of America

Readers should be aware that Internet Web sites offered as citations and/or sources for further information may have been changed or disappeared between the time this was written and when it is read.

DANIEL:
A LIFE TRANSFORMED
LISA CULVERWELL

PUBLISHED by PARABLES
Earthly Stories with a Heavenly Meaning

TABLE OF CONTENTS

Foreword	8
Chapter 1 - Who Is Daniel?	10
Chapter 2 - The Accident	21
Chapter 3 - The Fires	25
Chapter 4 - The Diagnosis	29
Chapter 5 – Changes	35
Chapter 6 – Deliverance	41
Chapter 7 - Daniel's Deliverance	51
Chapter 8 - Only the Beginning	71

LISA CULVERWELL

DANIEL: A LIFE TRANSFORMED

Foreword

Daniel was a little boy from a broken family that struggled to get along with others and let his fists settle too many disagreements. In his 20's, he started dealing drugs and landed himself in prison. He spent his 30's working for the family business, while viewing women as objects, using them for sex. He was a man who lived a life on the edge for most of his life. He was into many different things that most would say would make life more difficult, but Daniel would shrug it off and claim that it made his life more enjoyable. He was into alcohol, drugs, prostitution, just to name a few. He was in prison for a short while for distribution of drugs and possession of illegal weapons. Most knew him for his

LISA CULVERWELL

sarcasm, "in-your-face" comments, pure hate for anyone different from him, and "I don't care what you think" attitude. He would say what was on his mind, no matter how rude or vulgar it was. You see, Daniel was probably known as your typical American that loved life so much, but it didn't always love him.

This is the recount about a man who loved life but hated the world. But it doesn't end there. No! This was a man who hated nearly everyone and was into so many dark things, then birthed a man who loved, was kind, was no longer vulgar, and loved God most of all. His life was changed in an instant, and with this life-change came reflection and a life changed so much that friends no longer recognized him.

This recount is about the Daniel he was and the profound change that took place that changed everything about him.

DANIEL: A LIFE TRANSFORMED

CHAPTER 1
WHO IS DANIEL?

Daniel, a man from California, was a man who many thought was sarcastic, who laughed at his own misunderstood jokes yet didn't quite get the jokes of others, a man with a huge personality that couldn't be quelled, and someone that was extremely careless. That was what all of his friends saw, which was, for the most part, spot on. What his friends didn't see was his dark side.

Daniel was a man who loved everything material and anything that would give him an adrenaline rush. Life lessons taught him about certain highs that would get him in severe trouble. Those life lessons changed slightly to much more satisfying highs that were fleeting.

As a boy, Daniel experienced life as so many other young boys do in America – in a broken family with a single parent. As his mother left his brother (my husband, Maurice) and him at very young ages, it left him with a lot of questions. There were stories about why she left, but they are all different and will probably remain unconfirmed. We will never know whether this was the reason why Daniel was the way he was. Whatever the reason, he was a true rebel in every sense of the word, from learning a new word and waiting until company was at the house to start screaming it while jumping on his bed, to fighting anyone that he felt wronged him. Growing up, he found himself in trouble quite often. Unfortunately, this would dictate how he would become in his adult years.

When he hit his 20's, drugs became a major part of his life. He became an extremely hateful person, hating anyone unlike him, whether someone was of a different nationality, different belief, or different sexuality. Anyone he met that was different from him in nearly every way, he would make sure they knew how he felt. He had slang for every different nationality and sexuality, all-the-while he felt he was a Christian and that God hated them as much as he did. He hated so much that he had a swastika tattooed on his arm. He wanted to be a part of the KKK so badly and agreed with their beliefs wholeheartedly. It's no wonder he didn't get himself killed on numerous occasions!

He moved out of his father's house and into a house up north, where drugs were prevalent. He began doing drugs occasionally and started selling drugs on a normal basis. All those in the drug world knew him up there and knew that he could sell an air conditioner to an Eskimo. They all claimed to be his friends, but Daniel knew that if drugs weren't involved, he didn't matter to them. He did manage to make one friend that didn't care if drugs were involved or not. An unfortunate incident happened where Daniel was helping a friend move and his friend's sister was angry at her brother. She put a box with drugs, a grenade, and gun powder in the door of Daniel's van and called in a tip to the local police. They were both at a mall in Redding when the police arrived along with the bomb squad, treating it as a bomb threat. They had to evacuate everyone at the mall because of this "tip" his friend's sister called in.

They both went to prison, which of course hardened Daniel all the more. Because of Daniel's view of skin color, the prison was forced to put him in a separate wing with only white people, based on Daniel's word that he would kill anyone who was placed in a cell with someone who wasn't white. Knowing exactly how and why they found drugs in the door of his van and knowing they weren't his, Daniel got messages across the prison where they held his friend. He had stated that if his friend didn't tell the warden what actually happened and the drugs had nothing to do with Daniel, he would find a way to mess him up, or worse, kill him. I guess that message was heard loud and clear, since Daniel was released soon there after. As a part of his restitution, he was required to work and pay for everything that had happened. Fortunately, his dad was able to put him to work as the route driver for the family business.

    Having been in prison for a short while hardened Daniel in a big way. Maurice loved pushing Daniel's buttons and knew exactly what to do to set him off. Daniel didn't like having his buttons pressed and when they were, Daniel began threatening Maurice's life. When the threat of police being called was announced, Daniel's response was not a good one. After his experience with being taken into custody and taken to prison, the police were the last people he wanted called and he was willing to do whatever it took to make sure that didn't happen, even if it meant forcibly silencing his brother.

    Once he hit his 30's, he seemed to calm down a bit. He still had his attitude, but at

DANIEL: A LIFE TRANSFORMED

least he had steady employment working for his dad in the family business. He had given up on drugs, both using and selling, but still managed to find women that always used, whether drugs, alcohol, or both. No matter who he met, they were always the wrong choice. Most of them were married, on drugs, or prostitutes; only a few were good women. I remember walking by his phone, one day, after he had received a text. I happened to glance down at it while the text was still lit up in the notifications. I have to tell you, I can never un-see what I saw on his phone that day. He received constant emails and phone calls from various women he'd met on Craigslist or other online sites. We thought he may have been with up to 40-50 women. We later learned it was hundreds. We were shocked. The stories I heard about the person Daniel was before I met him were astonishing and disturbing.

    I met him when he was 33 years old, after his brother, Maurice, was in an accident and I moved to California to take care of him. He came off as arrogant, self-absorbed, cruel, and absolutely hateful. I didn't know what his past had entailed, but I thought whatever it was had to be bad. In my life, I had experienced people that were hateful, but no one came close to Daniel.

    Since I was always back-and-forth from the house to the hospital, I didn't see much of Daniel and couldn't get to know him very easily. I saw him occasionally, but when I did, it was always very interesting. One day, after Maurice was released from the hospital, Daniel and I went to the local hamburger joint to pick up dinner for everyone, which gave us a little bit of time to get to know each other. When we got back to his dad's house, where we were staying, Daniel asked us for some mustard. Not knowing his personality real well, I threw some mustard packets at him, expecting him to see me throw them and catch them. He didn't catch them – they hit him instead. I found out just how lucky I was that day. Daniel's demeanor was that if you threw something at him, as a joke or as I did, he would go to the extreme and throw something much bigger back. In other words, I was lucky he didn't grab a mustard bottle and empty it on my head. At one time, Maurice threw some candy at him as a joke. Daniel came back and threw the bowl and all the candy in it at Maurice. Instead of dodging a few pieces of candy, he was dodging a glass bowl and all of its contents, and Daniel thought this was hilarious.

DANIEL: A LIFE TRANSFORMED

As my and Maurice's relationship continued to grow, we would get into the occasional argument. Daniel always had a horrible habit of putting himself in the middle of our argument by telling me why I was wrong and Maurice was right. He always felt the need to give his opinion about our arguments, no matter how wrong or hurtful they were.

Once Maurice was well enough and was able to work again, we decided it was best for us to move out of his dad's house and get a place of our own. We moved about a hundred miles south of where his family was living. Daniel would come to visit every so often and I didn't mind. We had enough time apart from him that it didn't bother me. All I knew was that Maurice and Daniel would stay up all night working on model airplanes and Daniel would sleep on the couch. Our cat, Nadia, loved him and couldn't get enough of him. Daniel always had a way with animals. As hateful as he was with people, he was the most loving with animals.

I married Maurice in 2009 and the only person to come to our tiny wedding was my mother. We had such a bad relationship with his side of the family that we really didn't want anyone else there. We had friends at our reception, but still no family, other than my mother.

After a couple of years, we moved back up north to Napa. Their dad called and told us he wanted to retire from the family business and wanted us to run it, and he would help us purchase our home if we moved. Of course, this meant that we would be around Daniel a lot more often. We began working for the family business and things started off well, but in the end, it all ended very badly. Although Daniel and I grew closer in our "relationship", the relationship we had with the rest of the family grew apart and shattered into a million pieces. We left the family business, which was somewhat mutual, but very dramatic. We left there with so much hate in our hearts for the family that it was impenetrable.

Shortly after we left the family business, Daniel moved in with us and brought a dog with him by the name of Keek. By this time, the relationship I had with Daniel was much more pleasant, especially since we had a mutual love for animals. Daniel and I had a love/hate relationship at times. Actually, you could truly describe it as a brother/sister relationship. He'd annoy me and I'd yell or lecture at him… you know how it is. Even though our relationship was better, he still had that bad habit of intervening his opinion into every argument. He also had a way of getting Maurice to agree with things Daniel was saying to me and about me. This caused a lot of tension between Maurice and I, who, at this point, had only been married for four years. It nearly ended my marriage with Maurice. I had packed everything I could think of in a small trailer and my car with every intention of moving back to Ohio, where I'm from. It took a couple of days of talking before I finally realized that Maurice made me a better person, but also that Maurice realized what he had been doing to me and that it was because of his brother. We both asked Daniel to leave – he had a few weeks to find a place of his own. When Daniel saw what was happening and that he was a major part of the problem, he obliged and moved once he found a place he could call home.

After he finally moved out, it was so nice being able to see him when I wanted to see him. It gave Maurice and I a chance to repair what was broken and work on our marriage. It gave Maurice the ability to think before he spoke when we were around his brother.

LISA CULVERWELL

Chapter 2
The Accident

Daniel was the route driver for the family business. Every morning like clockwork, he would show up to work between 7:00 A.M. – 8:00 A.M. to collect orders out for delivery and this day started out like any other. That afternoon, Daniel was sitting at a red light when a young man driving a limo rear-ended him going roughly 35mph. Daniel saw the accident coming and stood on the brake petal, which arguably was not the best idea.

Daniel continued to work, even though each day brought him more back pain. He finally went to the doctor and they discovered he had a few herniated discs and it was directly caused by the accident.

LISA CULVERWELL

Daniel went on temporary disability, thinking he would be back to work within a few months, but he ended up needing back surgery to fuse his vertebrae together, causing him to be off from work much longer than anticipated. Unfortunately, the pain didn't end there. Over the course of months, even years, he continued to be in severe pain that none of the doctors could pinpoint. In the beginning, doctors would look at the MRI results and couldn't figure out why he was in as much pain as he was.

Doctor after doctor, referral after referral, out of all of the doctors he saw, there was only one specialist outside of his insurance that looked and stated that there was a lot of damage done from the accident and recommended either another surgery or nerve blockers. After giving all of this evidence to his current doctor, he got nowhere. Actually, they discounted the evidence completely and stated that they were refusing to do another surgery on him, claiming that they were requiring him to live out the rest of his life in pain. After this final incident, Daniel was finally told what to do to make things happen within the medical center. After contacting their customer care center, he was finally able to see a different doctor within his network.

DANIEL: A LIFE TRANSFORMED

After receiving the same answer every time he spoke with his regular doctor, he finally decided to do something about it and switch. This doctor was spot on with getting further imaging appointments immediately. Daniel was sent in to have another MRI done to look for any changes in his spine. The doctors thought they saw something and ordered he go in for a CT-scan. Daniel's life was forever changed the very next day…

LISA CULVERWELL

Chapter 3
The Fires

In 2017, we had massive fires burn through a large portion of Napa County as well as Sonoma County throughout Sonoma and Santa Rosa. These devastating fires made many people homeless in Santa Rosa. Napa had quite a bit of devastation as well, but not nearly to the effect of our neighboring county. We were awakened by our emergency line through our HOA at 12:30 A.M. on October 9th with a mandatory evacuation order. This isn't easy for most people, especially at that time of night, but we had two dogs (one of which was a puppy, only a few months old) and two cats that we needed to collect. We were blessed in that we had quite a bit of time to collect materials that we knew was important and that each one of our beloved pets were all in the house, making it easy to collect them all. We didn't know where to go immediately, so we went to my office. There, we had my computer to keep us up to date on what was happening and how bad it truly was. Later in the morning, Daniel was the first person we contacted. Without hesitation, he took us in for nearly two weeks. We were so grateful for what he did for us and we all ended up taking care of each during that time. Thankfully, no one in our neighborhood lost anything! The first responders were lifesavers in every aspect of the word, and then some.

    Daniel's apartment was essentially a converted garage underneath a house. This normally wouldn't be an issue, except it was below water level and he lived right next to the Napa River. Napa County had red-tagged his apartment after being reported by some disgruntled neighbors that had been forced to leave. His landlord was always making excuses for why he couldn't leave the apartment. It wasn't until immediately after the fires that he found out from the county that he had to be out by October 31st or they would force him out. It was just two short weeks after we were cleared to go home that he moved back in with us.

This time, Daniel moving in was different for all of us. We needed him as badly as he needed us; we needed him financially (Maurice is disabled and no longer on temporary disability) and he needed a home. He quickly moved what he had back into our home, back into the room he had been staying in previously.

Daniel and Maurice always had a mutual love for flying model airplanes. They both loved flying them, but Maurice equally loved building them. This was a typical night for Maurice whereas he would go to the garage and start building, when he could. His disability causes him so much pain that he can only stand to be in the garage for an hour or two at most. Daniel was never a very good builder. He always thought he could build and compared himself to Maurice constantly, always thinking he was as good a builder as his brother, if not better. As good a builder as Daniel thought he was, every time he'd crash an airplane, he was very quick to bring it to Maurice to fix. Maurice, for the most part, obliged to fix the broken down airplanes for Daniel, but sometimes he just wanted to build something for himself or even a new build for a friend. It wasn't always easy when Daniel would "borrow" something from the garage and never put it back or put it somewhere else. Maurice spent a lot of his time looking for his stuff or sifting through messes that Daniel had left.

    Maurice very quickly discovered he no longer had the "Patience of Job", as others claimed he had, and it took everything he had in him not to start throwing things at him at times. Daniel would make off-the-wall comments to him that was uncharacteristic even for Daniel. He had made a comment in the garage, one time, to Maurice that neither one of us could believe. He said, "If I were one of your friends, you would've helped me, already." Maurice never told him that he wouldn't help, he simply asked Daniel if he could wait because he was in the middle of something else. There was something going on underneath that we knew nothing about, and Daniel wasn't talking about it with anyone. But with me this time, something happened… something in him changed. Other than the typical Daniel, leaving things lay around the house, he tried not to annoy me for some reason. For the first time, we were there for each other.

Chapter 4
The Diagnosis

Daniel's dad started going to a church regularly and began talking with Daniel about it. He also talked about healing events with his healer. We were extremely leery about what was being said and immediately thought that it was a cult. Daniel was talking about everything their dad had told him and we were amazed by how fake it sounded. We kept telling Daniel that we didn't feel that it was safe for him to talk to his dad about this any longer. We knew that with Daniel being slightly gullible, he would believe these things. During this time, he started attended a church that I had wanted to try out for quite a while. He began going every Sunday and we began to see small changes in him, but nothing really significant. He had been going to this church for a couple of months. We finally started going to this church and we really enjoyed it and I had considered becoming a member. During this time, their dad continued to talk about these healing events and got Daniel to go to one. They eventually went to Arizona to the Arizona Deliverance Center and Daniel came back changed, even more so than before. The changes we discovered in him were pretty big – he was, of course, still talking about all of this, but this time he cleaned up his foul language and the way he viewed everything, and was no longer hateful… at all! There was one thing that didn't quite change though, he was shoving all of this stuff down our throats and he didn't care if it offended us. Typical Daniel would get in your face and tell you what he felt he wanted or needed to tell you and didn't care if you wanted to hear it or not.

We just wanted him to stop, but he wouldn't! We were both already Christians who had accepted our Lord and Savior, but we were taking the stance of someone who didn't have or want God in their lives. If we joked around about the things Daniel was saying (Daniel doesn't convey things very well – he usually tells us something completely different than what actually happened), Daniel would throw an enormous fit and tell us he would force us to go to Arizona with him if we didn't shut up.

One afternoon, their dad sent Maurice a text asking him if he'd like to go to lunch with him. This was the first time his dad wanted to go to lunch with him, and of course we were wondering what was going on. Not only was this the first time his dad wanted to have lunch with his eldest son, but it was the first time they had contact with each other in quite some time. The last time they saw each other, it ended on a pretty bad note with Maurice storming out. They went to lunch for three hours and talked. Maurice said he didn't know who this man was. The man Maurice grew up with wasn't the same man he had lunch with; it felt as though he was an imposter. Maurice told me everything they talked about and said he really enjoyed their time together. Then he told me that his dad started talking about the healing events with him like he did with Daniel. It was then that we found out how different Daniel's account of everything was from his dad's. To Maurice, it all sounded like it made sense. I, on the other hand, was scared. I was scared I was losing my husband to a cult and I wasn't going to stand idly by and lose my husband. I was going to put up a fight! After that day, Daniel had finally started to quiet down about all of it... until that dreadful day.

On April 13, while I was on my lunchbreak, I got online and searched my social media profile to see what was going on with everyone. I came across a post from Daniel that stunned me, begging the question "where's the punch line?" The post read: "Well family and friends, yesterday I had a CT scan done because during my last MRI, they found spots on my liver. The CT scan showed me positive for advanced stage pancreatic cancer. Not what I wanted to hear as we all know this cancer is a killer for men!!! Love all of you and by God's hand, I will be healed. I really need God's miracle right now, but perhaps it's time to go home." Needless to say, there was no punchline.

We all went out to dinner that evening to discuss Daniel's diagnosis. Being Daniel's sister-in-law, I immediately began telling him that he needed to listen to the doctors and do whatever they told him to do. Better yet, go to one of these hospitals that specialize in cancer treatments. Each word I said caused him to lash out at me quicker

DANIEL: A LIFE TRANSFORMED

than I could get the words out. He snapped at me and told me that there was only one person in the world "qualified" to pray for him, no other prayers worked, and that my prayers wouldn't save him. God didn't listen to anyone else, only this individual. I nearly ran out of the building crying at that moment, because all I had done since finding out about his cancer was pray. I knew he was lashing out and that he didn't mean it, but it still hurt all the same. Ultimately he apologized, but he adamantly thought that only one person was qualified to speak to God for him. It was then that I thought the best thing I could do, at that point, was to keep my mouth shut. We needed to be supportive of every decision he made, regardless of what that decision was. He had decided at that moment that he wasn't going to have any treatments done. When he had done research that day, he discovered that with his type of cancer, chemo typically shortened the life span even more than his life was being shortened already, and we agreed.

When we went to leave the restaurant, Maurice told me that Daniel wanted us to go to a healing event with him. I threw a huge fit and put my foot down. I said I wasn't going to lose my husband to some stupid cult and I wouldn't let him go. He disagreed and argued about how this wasn't a cult and pleaded that I go with him. He said he was going to go with or without me, but he'd really like me there. This was the only way Daniel was willing to spend time with his family. Out of support for Daniel, I sucked it up and went for him. When we got there, my in-laws were there and it took everything in me to not walk out of the building to avoid them. I wanted nothing to do with them; I still had so much hate for them. I sat down, crossed my arms, and had this look on my face so that everyone would know I wanted nothing to do with this. Dr. Susan Richards presided over this healing event. She started talking about testimonies of people that God had healed through her – she was talking about every detail of their illnesses. When she began to pray, there were people falling asleep – I had never been in a prayer where someone prayed for over an hour… I was falling asleep! I just wanted out of there. I wanted nothing to do with this stuff. Little did I know that all of this "stuff" was our saving grace.

Chapter 5
Changes

Shortly following Daniel's cancer diagnosis, he made the decision to go to church with his dad. He felt the need to be with his dad, and I really didn't blame him. Once he went, he felt that the services and prayer were much deeper than the other church; he felt that he was getting more out of the new church. He began praying more and I actually saw him reading a Bible. He had never owned a Bible before, let alone read one. As a little boy, they taught him all of the famous Bible stories in Sunday school, so this truly was new to him. He didn't know anything more about the Bible. Even when I would explain the Old Testament to him, he refused to believe that God was a jealous

God and certainly didn't believe the Old Testament. Reading the Bible opened his eyes and really did make an even greater change in him.

One late afternoon, Daniel came home and started talking about it again, and my thought was "Oh no, here we go again. Please just SHUT UP!" He said something to me that will forever impact my life. "God told me to tell you that if you repent of all of your sins, great things will happen to you." My immediate response was "Are you telling me God's accusing me of lying? I repent all the time!" Daniel's response was, "I'm just telling you what God told me to tell you. Take it as you will." That day, we had the longest conversation up to that point. We talked about God, beliefs, repenting, and what Daniel wanted from life.

When I went to bed, I thought about what Daniel had said, so I starting praying and said to God, "God, you're right. I don't repent every day like I'm supposed to." I didn't repent like I normally would. Typically, I would forget and repent only when something reminded me, like an accident – something would scare me into repenting. No, this time, I immediately began repenting about absolutely everything I could think of. That night, he kept putting people in my dreams to pray for... in groups... all night long. I was praying for people I couldn't possibly know... for their sins, their healing, and for them in general. I woke up a different person than I was when I went to bed the night before.

I told both Daniel and Maurice my experience and also spoke with the pastor at the church Maurice and I had been attending. I told him about the church and said that they seemed radical. I wanted to verify whether or not what they were practicing was a cult or not. He stated that within Christianity, there is a broad spectrum of beliefs. He said on the far-left spectrum, you have the radical Christians that believe that they can heal, cast out demons, and raise the dead. On the far-right spectrum, you have Christians that believe that since Jesus was "homeless" and lived on the streets without food or drink, they should, therefore, also live the same way... homeless, on the streets, and going hungry (I, personally, had never heard of Christians like this). He said the spectrum in the middle are all other Christians. He said the way they believe is absolutely Christian and is absolutely not a cult. He asked me why I thought this was a cult and I explained to him about being taught that we can't do any of the things they claim we can and why. He asked me, "Why do you think we don't have the ability to do supernatural things?" I stated that it was because the Bible states that we can't – those supernatural powers died with Jesus' disciples and we're not supposed to have those powers. He then asked me, "Where, in the Bible, does it support that fact?" He said that most churches teach this, but there's nothing that supports this fact in the Bible. Traditional churches, we've discovered, water down the Bible. In Matthew 28:19-20, it says "Go therefore and make disciples of all the nations, baptizing them in the name of the Father and of the Son and of the Holy Spirit, teaching them to observe all things that I have commanded you, and lo, I am with you always, even to the end of the age." Traditional churches teach us that when Jesus and his disciples all died, the power of God within them died. This means that the power of God cannot be within anyone else besides them. There's no evidence in the Bible that suggests this. In Matthew 28:20, it says "teaching them to observe all things that I have commanded you", which suggests that when Jesus was alive, he taught his disciples that they would all have the power to heal, cast out demons, and raise the dead through Jesus' name when the Holy Spirit was to come upon them in the Upper Room. Wouldn't that also suggest that if they were all taught to do these things in His name, they too would go out to teach us all?

The first major change that took place in our lives was that we were reunited with Maurice and Daniel's father and stepmother. These were the people whom we hadn't spoken to in over five years! These were the people we had garnered such hate for and hurt for so long! We called their dad and I spoke with him myself. After about 30 minutes, I hung up the phone. Maurice asked me if I recognized the man I spoke with and I said "NO!" He said "I told you!" He was a completely changed man that I needed to get to know... one that I hadn't ever known before.

The next day, and a couple more times after that, I was delivered from all evil (I will explain this in more detail a little later). Suddenly, all of these changes started happening that I, and all of us, could visibly see. My attitude changed, I had patience where I had none, I felt love for everyone no matter their belief, I was suddenly bold and wanted to shout it from the rooftops, and so many more things! He started putting people in my mind every day to pray for. He never told me why, He just told me to pray for this person and be specific… like pray for comfort. Later on, I would find out that the person I prayed for was going through something pretty big… every time. Soon after, Maurice started going through some of the same things. In this time, we switched from going to the church that Daniel had been going to and began going to the church his dad and stepmom went to. You see, I'm telling you all of this because it was all because of Daniel.

Chapter 6
Deliverance

One of the things that we, as Christians need to do is be delivered. What is a deliverance? The best way to describe it is that's it's an exorcism. You see, everyone can have demons and evil spirits, but it depends of whether or not the person is saved if the person is infected or tormented. A person that has not been saved can be demonized by a demon, or in worst-case scenario they can be possessed. A person who is saved is tormented by a demon or evil spirit. The difference is that a possession means that you are owned by something and to be demonized means that they don't own you yet they have control, whereas tormenting means it doesn't own you and it doesn't take control of your

body. It uses your thoughts to convince you that something is a good idea. Examples of this would be:
- Pornography
- Gambling
- Alcoholism
- Drugs
- Fornication
- Sleeping with someone of the same sex

A demon can also torment you with the use of pain and illness. Examples of this are:
- Alzheimer's
- Fibromyalgia
- Migraines
- Stomach issues
- Bad joints
- Death

In Daniel's case, a demon caused the cancer and made it spread like wild fire, causing him discomfort, sickness, and loss of weight. This was presented to us in his deliverance video.

Demons enter us when we're most vulnerable… while we're still in our mother's womb. While our body is being created, Satan uses that as an opportunity to infuse himself with us. Have you ever noticed that children inherently know how to lie or to do the opposite of what they're told? They may not know right from wrong at that stage, but there's a reason why they know how to do that without ever being shown how. Satan. He laid the groundwork. If Satan didn't "infuse" himself, we'd all be perfect. We wouldn't know how to sin. Whether or not demons would have the ability to enter us at a later time, that I don't know, but it's because of Satan that all of the groundwork was placed and we're all in the position we're in!

How do demons and evil spirits enter the body and mind post-birth? By our actions! If we lie, that can open the doors to demons. If we cheat or steal, that can open the doors to demons. If we decide it would be a good idea to watch pornography (although probably already because of a demon), that opens the door to a whole plethora demons. If we decide to have sexual relations with someone outside of marriage, that, too, opens the door to demons. When someone has multiple sexual partners, that person becomes "one in flesh" with the other person (think of it) like marriage – when you marry someone, the two become one in Christ. It's just like that when you sleep with someone outside of marriage – the two become one in Satan). My mother used to say to me, "Every person you sleep with leaves a little piece of them behind." Little did she know how true she actually was! In other words, every person someone sleeps with opens the door to a plethora of possible demons to enter into them... each person. So if someone sleeps with 10 people, you've just opened the door to a multitude of demons. This can happen in other ways as well: gambling, addiction, gluttony, movies (horror and killing), even through our family members. There are demons called "Soul-Ties" where they have every right to be in your body through generational curses. For example, I had two great-grandfathers, one on each side, that were both alcoholics and were very angry and abusive when they were drunk. One did things to his children and the other threatened to kill my grandfather with the shotgun. Both of them instilled fear in his children. That fear was a generational curse, or soul-tie, that was passed down to me. I had fear at every turn I made, always wondering if someone was watching me or was about to hurt me. There was never anyone there, but it always felt like it. I had always thought I was just paranoid or it was from <u>watching bits and pieces of those horror movies on Halloween</u> as a child. Not only did I get the soul-tie from both great-grandfathers, I opened the door to even worse ones from watching those little bits and pieces of horror movies. I found myself always afraid the shower nozzle was going to come down and strangle me – that came from one of the horror movies.

A deliverance is something that should be done before being baptized in water; it's essentially a baptism of the soul. You see, when you're being baptized, it's best that you are cleansed completely. The water baptism cleanses you and makes you whole in spirit, but it doesn't cleanse your body. In other words, when you're baptized, you want to make sure that all impure thoughts, impure actions, addictions, etc. are removed. This way, when you're baptized, you have a clean mind, body, and soul.

Many of you probably think that deliverance is not biblical. I can assure you it is – deliverance, or the casting out of demons, is actually talked about in the Bible more than 20 times. Here are some bible verses to help prove that deliverance is biblical:

1. Psalm 32:7 – You are my hiding place; you will protect me from trouble and surround me with songs of deliverance.

2. Psalm 34:4 – I sought the LORD, and he answered me; he delivered me from all

my fears.

3. Psalm 34:17 – The righteous cry out, and the LORD hears them; he delivers them from all their troubles.

4. Psalm 107:6 – Then they cried out to the LORD in their trouble, and he delivered them from their distress.

5. 2 Corinthians 10:3-4 – For though we live in the world, we do not wage war as the world does. The weapons we fight with are not the weapons of the world. On the contrary, they have divine power to demolish strongholds.

6. Matthew 10:8 – Heal the sick, raise the dead, cleanse those who have leprosy, drive out demons. Freely you have received; freely give.

In Mark 5, it talks about an impure spirit that was inside of a man that came to Jesus. Mark 5 says, "They went across the lake to the region of the Gerasenes. When Jesus got out of the boat, a man with an impure spirit came from the tombs to meet him. This man lived in the tombs, and no one could bind him anymore, not even with a chain. For he had often been chained hand and foot, but he tore the chains apart and broke the irons on his feet. No one was strong enough to subdue him. Night and day among the tombs and in the hills he would cry out and cut himself with stones. When he saw Jesus from a distance, he ran and fell on his knees in front of him. He shouted at the top of his voice, 'What do you want with me, Jesus, Son of the Most High God? In God's name don't torture me!' For Jesus had said to him, 'Come out of this man, you impure spirit!' Then Jesus asked him, 'What is your name?' 'My name is Legion,' he replied, 'for we are many.' And he begged Jesus again and again not to send them out of the area. A large herd of pigs was feeding on the nearby hillside. The demons begged Jesus, 'Send us among the pigs; allow us to go into them.' He gave them permission, and the impure spirits came out and went into the pigs. The herd, about two thousand in number, rushed down the steep bank into the lake and were drowned."

Mark 1:23-25 says, "Just then a man in their synagogue who was possessed by an impure spirit cried out, 'What do you want with us, Jesus of Nazareth? Have you come to destroy us? I know who you are – the Holy One of God!' 'Be quiet!' said Jesus sternly. 'Come out of him!' The impure spirit shook the man violently and came out of him with a shriek." Matthew 8:28-34 states the same as Mark 1:23-25. Matthew 12:22 says, "Then they brought him a demon-possessed man who was blind and mute, and Jesus healed him, so that he could both talk and see." In Mark 9:38-41 says, "'Teacher,' said John, 'we saw someone driving out demons in your name and we told him to stop, because he was not one of us.' 'Do not stop him', Jesus said. 'For no one who does a miracle in my name can in the next moment say anything bad about me, for whoever is not against us is for us. Truly I tell you, anyone who gives you a cup of water in my name because you belong to the Messiah will certainly not lose their reward." There are many more verses like the ones I provided you. Not only could Jesus heal the sick and drive out demons from the possessed, so could his disciples. The last verse I gave you states that all men could do the same, in the name of Jesus Christ.

There are three things you must do in order to be delivered. First, you must ask Jesus to be your Lord and Savior. Second, you must ask for forgiveness from God and others. Third, you <u>must</u> forgive. You can't ask for forgiveness all while refusing to forgive others. You must let go of <u>all</u> grudges against others. Trust me, it's the most difficult thing to do, I know. But to forgive is for you, not for them! When you forgive, you are free.

You must release everything to God – all of your anger, guilt, hurt, worry, and control. You must let it all go!

When you sit down initially before your deliverance, you are asked what sins you've committed. In other words, what evil spirits and/or demons are in you. They make a list of everything as you tell them so that they make sure they've gotten rid of everyone. Plus it allows them to call each one out by name and talk to them (yes, I said talk to them, not at or with) – yes, as crazy as that sounds, they speak. When doing a deliverance, it's never a good idea to cast out demons without demanding to speak to them. Not talking to them provides the demons a way to stay and hide in the shadows. When you speak to them, you learn who is there so you know who to bind. Typically, you're not going to be able to get them all in one deliverance. There can be multiple demons by the same name, so when you cast out one, there may be another not presented until later.

LISA CULVERWELL

DANIEL: A LIFE TRANSFORMED

Chapter 7
Daniel's Deliverance

Daniel found out about a pastor in Florida, Pastor Mark, that did deliverances. Daniel's dad also did deliverances, but he felt that Pastor Mark had been doing them much longer, had more knowledge, and dug deeper than others, so the choice for him to go to Pastor Mark was obvious. Daniel's dad lent him the money to purchase a plane ticket and was absolutely ecstatic about going, which was scheduled for May 6.

Daniel had never been to Florida before, so his first experience was definitely memorable for him. He was amazed at how humid it was there and the fact that the palm trees in Florida actually grow coconuts. He was able to rent a jet ski for a short time and see the Atlantic Ocean for the very first time. He felt as though he was already in Heaven! On May 7, Daniel went to see Pastor Mark for his deliverance.

Daniel's deliverance provided us with a lot of information, some made us say "Oh, that's what he meant". Other information made us wish we never had knowledge of it. Because I want Daniel's remembrance to stay intact without soiling his memory, I'm not going to go into complete detail, as some of what we learned was difficult for his family to hear. I can only imagine, if it was difficult for his family, it would be that difficult, if not more so, for his friends who may be reading this.

Before doing a deliverance, Pastor Mark has a questionnaire that each individual must fill out – this questionnaire is extremely detailed and has 24 pages of questions for the individual to check. I must note that I had conversations with Pastor Mark and have received his blessing in sharing this confidential information. Pastor Mark felt that Daniel would want this to be made public-knowledge in order to help others that may have had the same experiences and may be wrestling with the same demons as he did all his life. The family is also on agreeance to share this information. Prior to Daniel's deliverance, he wouldn't share anything. Post deliverance, he was willing to share information on many things. On the questionnaire, Daniel had stated:

1. He was a Born-again Christian and that his relationship with God was good.

2. His mother wasn't a part of their lives.

3. He had tattoos, which he regretted shortly after getting them.

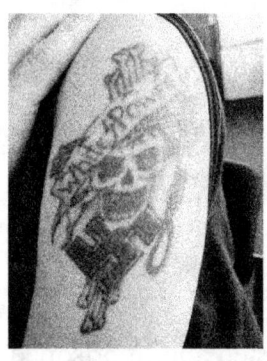
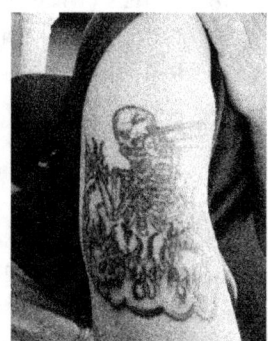

4. He was aware of having mental health issues (ADD/ADHD) and had been taking medication for them. If there were any other mental health issues, Daniel wasn't aware of them.

5. He was dealing with many emotional issues, such as:

    a. Abandonment
    b. Bitterness
    c. Guilt
    d. Insecurity
    e. Love (Difficulty receiving)
    f. Love (Difficulty giving)
    g. Stress
    h. Worthlessness, although he no longer felt this.

6. He had many addiction issues, such as:
    a. Drugs (illegal)
    b. Drugs (prescription)
    c. Pornography
    d. Sex
    e. Shoplifting
    f. Sleep Aids
    g. Social/Online Media
    h. Spending/Shopping
    i. Tobacco

7. He had been arrested and imprisoned for selling illegal drugs and theft.

8. He would choose physical beauty over other more important characteristics of women (although not any longer), but also desired to use women for sex.

9. He had many anger issues, such as:
    a. Emotional abuser
    b. Fighting (physical)

c. Fly off the handle
d. Frustration
e. Hatred
f. Physical abuser
g. Racism
h. Rage
i. Rebelliousness
j. Revenge
k. Un-forgiveness, noting he had come to peace with his un-forgiveness through Jesus.

10. He had several health issues, such as:
   a. Allergies
   b. Back Pain/Issues
   c. Cancer
   i. Diabetes
   ii. High Blood Pressure

11. He had witnessed a traumatic event from age 0-5:
   a. His mother left when he was 2 years old.

I wanted to tell you what he answered on his questionnaire because it would give you a glimpse of what we knew about him; however, there were things that we were told that we weren't prepared for.

Most that knew Daniel knew that he had an immense hate for others not like him, particularly those not of his own race, but also those not of his own sexuality. It was brought to our attention that this had all begun with someone that Daniel claimed had touched him inappropriately as a young child. This had opened a gateway for him that he found very difficult to control. Throughout his lifetime, he had been with hundreds of sexual partners and prostitutes. We discovered that Daniel was at war with himself; you are what you hate. He spent a great deal of time tearing down others for what they were doing, when in fact he was hating himself because he was, in fact, doing the same. We were told that he had multiple personalities, which we were, in a way, already aware of, and I'm sure many of his friends would feel that way as well. We knew, to some extent, some of those personalities and how they acted; however, there were also personalities that we weren't aware of. I wonder if, because of these multiple personalities, was he aware that he was doing the things he did?

Typically, Pastor Mark would have someone video the interview process. Unfortunately, that was not done with Daniel, otherwise I would possibly have more information to go off of.

Before the video started, deliverance took

DANIEL: A LIFE TRANSFORMED

place that involved his mother's "familiar spirit". A familiar spirit is one that comes from a person and is a demon. They lie and tell us what the person <u>may or may not</u> have been thinking or feeling, more than likely not. Pastor Mark also uses a scale to monitor how powerful manifestations (demons) are in a person based on how emotional the manifestation is. This is a 4-point "Richter scale" for deliverance. Pastor Mark stated that Daniel's manifestation of his mother's familiar spirit, as well as his hate, was one of the strongest he had encountered, measuring at a 3.2 and 3.5.

When a deliverance begins, the use of the Bible, the Cross, and Holy water are recommended, but not required. The Bible (represents a sword) is used to cut, or torment, the demon or evil spirit so that it wants to come out or to make it speak. Hebrews 4:12 says, "For the word of God is alive and active. Sharper than any double-edged sword, it penetrates even to dividing soul and spirt, joints and marrow, it judges the thoughts and attitudes of the heart." He tells the individual to go down, which basically means close your eyes or sleep. Pastor Mark tells the individuals to be with Jesus in order to help them feel comforted and relaxed, as they must have a clear mind. Doing so allows everything to take place without the individual intervening or fighting – we are told not to even pray as that will interrupt or even stop the deliverance. Once the individual has "gone to be with Jesus" or "goes down", a demon is told to come up. Sometimes it can take a while for this to happen, but Pastor Mark stated he was surprised at how quickly the demon manifested itself. Please note that what I'm about to share with you, this is only the second half of his deliverance and came directly from the video taken. This is the transcript from Daniel's recorded deliverance that follows:

Pastor Mark: "Satan, you're defeated!"

Satan: (With a huge smirk on his face and his voice was changed slightly) "You think so?"

Pastor Mark: "I know so. You want to know how I know? Because my Savior, Jesus, went to a cross for this man, shed His blood, gave up His spirit, for him to be healed. That's why I think so. You've done a pretty good job, though! I mean, since the beginning, Mom abandoning him at two years old, Mom didn't really love him, then all the drugs, the

DANIEL: A LIFE TRANSFORMED

alcohol, sex, the prostitution, you were this close to killing him! Aren't you???"

Satan: "Oh, we gave him cancer too!"

Pastor Mark: "Cancer of what?"

Satan: "Stage 4 pancreatic cancer. We figured that would be a good one to throw in there along with diabetes, heart problems, and asthma."

Pastor Mark: "Yeah, yeah, but you didn't count on one thing. And that's the spirit of his God to heal him. Did you put darts in the pancreas?"
Satan: "Yeah."

Pastor Mark: "You're going to start right now by removing those darts. Am I talking to Satan?" (Pastor Mark points his finger at Daniel and puts it on his chest. As he does so, Daniel jumps.) I talking to Satan?"

Satan: "No."

Pastor Mark: "Who am I talking to?" (The demon is making Daniel squirm.) "No. You may not move. Who am I talking to?"

Satan: "Lucifer." (Lucifer is also known as Satan, but they are two separate demons.)

Pastor Mark: "Is Satan there?"

Lucifer: "Yeah."

Pastor Mark: "Okay, Lucifer. Are you the one putting the cancer in the pancreas? Yes or no!"

Lucifer: "Yes."

Pastor Mark: "Take out the darts right now. Remove them, right now, remove them! Remove all your handy work from his pancreas right now. You're going to remove all the darts right now. Remove it all. Take it all out." (Darts are spiritual darts that demons put into certain organs to torment and cause pain or illness.)

(Fiery darts, or arrows, are the weapons that demons use to cause pain. They "insert" these arrows into various places to make us sick. By taking the arrows, or darts, out, it heals the pain or sickness.

Psalm 7:13 says, "He has prepared his

DANIEL: A LIFE TRANSFORMED

deadly weapons; he makes ready his flaming arrows."

Ephesians 6:16 says, "In addition to all this, take up the shield of faith, with which you can extinguish all the flaming arrows of the evil one."

(As Pastor Mark is telling Lucifer to remove all of the darts, it's forcing Daniel to physically remove all of the fiery darts from various places of the body.)

Lucifer: "We put it in his liver, too."

Pastor Mark: "Remove it from the liver."

Lucifer: "It's spreading like wild fire in him."

Pastor Mark: "Remove it."

(Daniel continues to pull out all of the fiery darts. As he does so, you can see the pain in his face.)

Pastor Mark: "Remove it all. Take it out. Take out all the cancer from his pancreas and from the liver. Remove it. It's all going to be gone. Take it all out. Take out the asthma, take out the diabetes. Whatever you put in his body, whatever devices you put in his body that caused that sickness, take it all out right now. Take it all out right now, remove it all. He's going to be free from this cancer when we finish here today. You're going to the pit and he's going to be set free from what you've been doing. Take it all out, Lucifer."

(You can hear Daniel wincing from the pain. This was actually Daniel, not the demon.)

Pastor Mark: "Take it all out. Every last bit of it, take it all out."

(Pastor Mark takes his "sword", the Bible, in a downward motion on Daniel's abdomen.)

Pastor Mark: "Take it all out. I remove it all. And all that sickness I bind to you, Lucifer. Now Lucifer, I'm done with you. You go down." (Go down means to go to sleep.) "Satan, get up. Get up, Satan." (Pastor Mark slaps the Bible on Daniel's chest and he's wakes in surprise.) "Are you the chief spirit here, Satan? Yes or no."

Satan: "Yes."

DANIEL: A LIFE TRANSFORMED

Pastor Mark: "You're defeated and you know it. You weren't counting on this."

Satan: "No."

Pastor Mark: "Yes. It is finished! That's what He cried out on the cross, "It Is Finished.""

(The facial expression seen on Daniel is actually the demon looking like he's going to cry in fear.)

Pastor Mark: "Who else is there with you, who else?"

Satan: "Jezebel (the demon of lust), Lust, Hate, Murder, Anger, Greed, Pride, Jealousy, Guilt, Pain, Inflammation, Homosexuality."

Pastor Mark: "Homosexual spirits there?"

Satan: "Yes."

Pastor Mark: "Did you get him to do it?"

Satan: "He helped."

Pastor Mark: "Okay, who else is there?"

LISA CULVERWELL

(Satan goes quiet about who else.)

Pastor Mark: "Any more important ones?"

Satan: "No."

Pastor Mark: "What about Racism?"

Satan: "Racism is just a small part."

Pastor Mark: "Well, he's there. What about the Nazi tattoo?"

Satan (giggling): "We fooled him into thinking that was cool."

Pastor Mark: "You sure did. Any Nazi spirits there?"

Satan: "Yes."

Pastor Mark: "Really? Is that his name, Nazi?"

Satan: "Yes."

Pastor Mark: "Any other Germanic spirits we should know about? Third-right spirits?

DANIEL: A LIFE TRANSFORMED

Holocaust spirits? Anything else?"

Satan: "No."

Pastor Mark: "Okay. I bind you Satan. I bind you. And all that sickness, I put on you. I put it all on you, right now. It's all bound to you, Satan."

Pastor Mark (makes Satan repeat after him): "I Satan, renounce all claims, to precious Daniel. We can't have him anymore. He doesn't belong to us. He was bought by the blood of his Savior. We failed in our assignment. I Satan, bind to me every devil under my authority. I bind to me Lucifer, Jezebel, and all the rest and I bind to me the pancreatic cancer, the diabetes, liver cancer, asthma, heart problems, and every other sickness is now bound to me.

(Satan has repeated all of what Pastor Mark demanded he repeat.)

Pastor Mark: "That's right, Satan. I take three or four cord in Ecclesiastes 4:12 and bind it all to you, Satan. All of his infirmities are bound to you, all those devils are bound to you, and you're going to take it all with you." (Pastor Mark smacks the Bible on Daniel's chest again, once again making him jump). "You're going to take it all with you. That's right, all those fiery darts you put in there are all removed. He's going to recover from it. The doctors won't understand what happened. He's going to make a full recovery, FULL REMISSION! It's all bound to you, Satan."

(Ecclesiastes 4:12 says, "Though one may be overpowered, two can defend themselves. A cord of three strands is not quickly broken."

Again, Pastor Mark makes Satan repeat after him.)

Pastor Mark: "Say I Satan, bound to my kingdom, bound to all the sicknesses. We go now… TO. THE. PIT! Out! Out! Go! Out! Come out!"

(As the demons and evil spirits leave the body, they go out through the mouth. This causes some to cough, yawn, spit, and even vomit. In Daniel's case, he coughed and yawned continuously until they were gone. The Bible is put on the back and the cross is placed on the head, all while Pastor Mark continuously tells them to leave.)

Satan (defeated): "Owe, we're leaving!"

(A trash can is placed in front of Daniel in case he vomits or needs to spit because physical deliverance can be extremely painful, as it uses every muscle in the body.)

(Once Pastor Mark sees that all of the demons and evil spirits are gone, he asks Holy Spirit to fill him.)

Pastor Mark: "Holy Spirit fill. Holy Spirit fill. Thank you Jesus. Every places filled with the devils, fill with the Holy Spirit. Thank you Jesus. Wherever the cells were infirmed, put Your Spirit there. Fill the pancreas. Fill the liver. Thank you Jesus. It's all over. Where the diabetes was, where the heart problems, fill them with your Holy Spirit. Thank you Jesus. I loose heal in the Name of Jesus. I command the organs to come into right working order right now in the Name of Jesus. Be healed in the Name of Jesus."

(Daniel is now calm, relaxed, praising God, and smiling. You can visibly see Daniel feels lighter and filled with the Holy Spirit.)'

What you just read is a typical deliverance; however, deliverances can much more violent, loud, and vulgar. I, myself, went through a second deliverance where Jezebel was cursing my father-in-law and was causing me to convulse and scratch the skin on my arms and legs. My father-in-law had to ask the angels to restrain the demon so as to not hurt myself or him. As painful, scary, and dramatic a deliverance can be, it's necessary to go through this to cleanse the spirit. Because you're filled with the Holy Spirit in the end, the feeling you have immediately after is absolutely nothing but love. It's not your typical love either. I beg to say that it's not even God's love that's felt, but only the love that Jesus felt for you while hanging on the cross. When I felt that unimaginable love, I was amazed I was able to stand up and walk toward my sister-in-law to give her a hug and tell her I love her and forgive her. After going through a deliverance, it can be impossible to walk or stand because you've used so many muscles and your breathing can be extremely heavy. In my case, I became light headed and everything from my head to my toes tingled. Please don't allow what I just shared to deter you from being delivered. It is so worth it to be closer to God.

LISA CULVERWELL

Chapter 8
Only the Beginning

Daniel came home from Florida a changed man. He had more love than I'd ever seen in him before! He was in constant prayer, in the Word, and had his worship music playing almost constantly. He posted on his social media about his healing and his experience in Florida. A few friends doubted him and what he was being told, suggesting that what he was being told was not of God. I, personally, can attest that it was God speaking to him because He spoke to me. Of course, both Maurice and I had a little doubt as well. Daniel took that our doubt was keeping him from being healed, but God had to speak to him and tell him that his faith was not in God if we had anything to do with his healing. God explained to him that he wasn't doing his part. You see, God heals all the time, but he expects you to do your part. A good example is if you're paralyzed from the waist down and God is telling you that you're healed. Do you expect God to do the physical therapy for you or do you do the physical therapy and let God handle the rest? That's what Daniel didn't understand – he thought God would do it all for him and he didn't have to do anything. Daniel started eating all the bad foods and drinks again that got him in this mess in the first place. He needed to eat healthy and stop drinking sugary sodas.

It was June 21, Daniel was in the hospital for nearly a week. That's when we realized that Daniel wasn't telling anyone just how bad his condition was. We heard it from the doctor. We went to see Daniel the day before he was released to tell him what the doctor told us. We had paperwork with us for him to sign; his dad had called him to tell him he needed to sign a medical directive, or a DNR and he agreed (at this time, his dad and stepmom were in Europe). We discovered that Daniel was snapping and berating the nurses. When a doctor would come to his room to tell him how bad he was and to get his affairs in order, he would get mad at them, tell them God's healed me and I'm going to live, and then proceed to talk to us about it like he was extremely angry about being told that by a doctor.

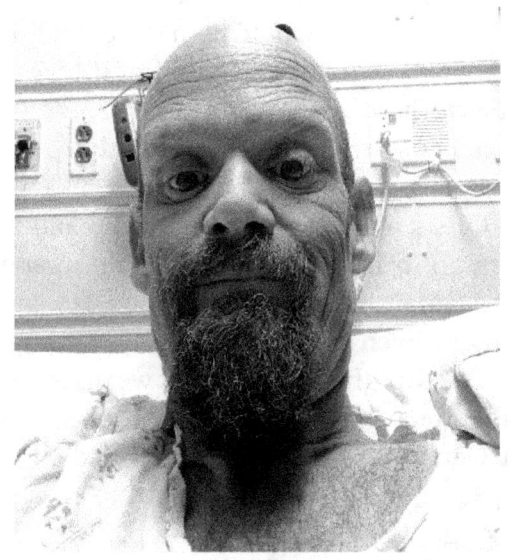

He was released on June 26 and drove himself to his dad's house. This caught his step-sister by surprise, as she was not expecting him to show up on her doorstep since his dad and step-mom were out of the country at the time. No one was expecting him to show up at their doorstep. Even we were surprised. We were expecting him to come back to our home. His step-sister was caring for her two very young children and her grandmother. Her grandmother tried to do everything for him, even though she can't speak English; she didn't have the patience, stamina, or strength to care for him. She was grateful when we would come over and help him, but she would still get upset if I tried to do the dishes (yes, even a scowl and taking dishes out of my hands translates the same in all languages).

On June 27, God spoke to me and told me to go to Daniel and allow Him to speak with Daniel directly through me. He said I wouldn't even know what He was going to say. This was the first time that we discovered that God gave me the give of prophecy. We met Daniel with the paperwork and for the next hour, God spoke to him through me. Although the entire conversation is a blur, He asked Daniel, "My child, why do you deny me?" We thought God would speak and Daniel would listen, but it turned out to be a conversation – Maurice and I were shocked! Daniel said he wasn't denying Him, but God said, "No, you don't deny me in the sense that I've saved you. You deny me by your actions. You're very angry. You're angry at me! You think I gave you cancer and I'm not taking it away. I didn't give you cancer, the enemy did. But I keep trying to take it away and you keep stopping it!" Every time someone would pray for him, he would turn away. This was noticed by other people in our church, as well. We don't know if it was out of embarrassment or if he still had some sort of demon in him that wouldn't allow him to accept prayer. The Lord told him to fall on his knees and give it all to Him. God said that part of the problem was that Daniel wasn't giving up control and he needed to give up ALL control. In the end, Daniel did just that. He gave up all control to God. God had me lay my hands on Daniel and tell him, "You are healed, my child! You will be in some discomfort and all of the impurities will come out of your pores, but don't be afraid for I am with you."

After the 27th, he was a changed man. He had joy and was willing to go through hell and back for Jesus. God told him that the impurities would come out from his pores and that's exactly what happened! He stayed up all night praising God and then noticed large puddles. He described it to me that he was sweating through his feet. When I saw him that night, he literally had streams pouring from his feet! I'd never seen anything like it! Everywhere he walked, he'd leave a large puddle. On the 29th, the cleaning lady came in and thought he was wetting himself because the fluid was yellow. He was extremely jaundice and what was coming out of him was bile, like a river. His legs and feet were extremely swollen to roughly three times their normal size. We thought this was God's prophecy being fulfilled! Because it was too difficult for his step-sister and her grandmother to care for him there, he came home with us on June 30th. It didn't take long for us to realize how difficult it was to care for him.

When he was in the hospital, they had prescribed him Oxycodone for the pain he was experiencing. Daniel had a problem with medication, just like with his spending habits. He couldn't budget his pills and would run out sooner than he should have. When he ran out of oxycodone, he began taking Norco, why is this important? Well, Maurice was looking through Daniel's room for more of Daniel's blood thinner shots when he came across a bag from the hospital that contained a note. It read:

1. Stop taking Norco immediately! Take the Oxycodone for pain.

2. Take the Lovanox shot twice a day.

DANIEL: A LIFE TRANSFORMED

3. Take two Sodium tablets three times a day.

4. Check blood-sugar twice a day.

5. Take blood-sugar medication, as needed.

When Maurice approached him about it, Daniel's response was, "Oh, I forgot", in typical Daniel fashion. You see, Norco has Tylenol in it that can damage the liver. When you're already in liver failure, Tylenol is the worst thing to take because it causes the liver to fail much faster.

He really couldn't do anything for himself. He grew weaker and we ultimately had to get a seated walker. He would get pushed to the bathroom or kitchen. We were thankful that the local hospital sent a wheelchair so he could be wheeled outside for some fresh air. We live in a rural part of Napa where it's very quiet. When you go outside, you hear the birds chirping, feel the warm sun and cool breeze on your face, and smell the clean air. Beautiful trees are all around us – absolutely nothing but God's beautiful creations are outside to bask in. We were so grateful that he could experience that when he did.

July 1, neither one of us went to church. We didn't realize how busy we would be and

LISA CULVERWELL

I didn't want to leave Maurice alone to care for his brother by himself. He needed help and rest, and I was going to do whatever it took to give it to him. Obviously, there were things a sister-in-law shouldn't be doing for her husband's brother. On one instance, we were all in the living room when Maurice asked Daniel if he needed to change his clothes. I thought he meant pants – after years of living with this man, I've seen him in his underwear more times than I can count. Not this time, no, Maurice meant underwear and all! Needless to say, I had a pillow in front of my face until they were finished. I really didn't ever want to need to un-see that!

On July 3, after only three days, Maurice realized that he wasn't able to care for his brother. He needed round-the-clock care that the hospital was giving him, and we just couldn't do it. Maurice had been trying to get in contact with his doctor about the Norco that Daniel had been taking after discovering the note. He had finally received a phone call from an on-call E.R. doctor and was told that Daniel should definitely not be taking the Norco. When Maurice explained that he couldn't physically care for Daniel, given his own physical condition, the doctor immediately put in a referral for hospice and

DANIEL: A LIFE TRANSFORMED

he received a phone call from them shortly thereafter.

On July 4, hospice came out so we could fill out the paperwork. We were surprised just how cooperative Daniel was with her. He willingly signed the paperwork and answered all of her questions. He was very forthcoming about how he wanted his affairs taken care of, but never mentioned himself. It wasn't about him. It was about God and his family, specifically his dog, Keek. He wanted to make sure that Keek was taken care of and knew he would always have a home here with us.

Daniel slowly walked out of the room to use the restroom and Maurice went to assist. I asked the woman from hospice a question: "Is it normal for him to leak fluids from his feet." Why I asked, I don't know since, to us, God had prophesied that it would happen before it started. I really wanted to hear that she'd never seen anything like it before; however, she said, "Yes. It's completely normal and we see it all the time. When the fluid builds up that badly, it has nowhere else to go but down. Gravity takes place and it comes out through the pores in the feet." My heart sank – I so wanted to hear the opposite. It was at that moment that a part of me knew what was next. She had stated that she never tells families how long she believes someone has when she meets them. She felt compelled to tell us that Daniel only had about a week remaining.

Maurice was in the kitchen preparing dinner (Maurice knew exactly how much to give him and what kind of food he could or should be eating) and I was in the living room with Daniel. Daniel had an app on his phone that played 6-7 hours of worship music and he would play this periodically. He turned the music on and as we were listening to it, the song "I Can Only Imagine" came on. I put my hand on his shoulder and told him that if he wants to see what Heaven looks like, listen to the words of this song. When I came back in the room, he had his hands held high to God, his face pointed towards Heaven, and a giant smile on his face. That's what he did whenever he listened to worship music – he fully worshipped. His mind, body, and soul were all craving to be in Heaven with the Lord Jesus.

Hospice had a hospital bed and a wheelchair delivered that night. Hospice wanted him in the bed, and so did we. We thought it was best for him with the issues he was facing. His right leg had been draining just fine; his left leg had just started draining. That night, he screamed pretty loudly in excruciating pain as his left leg cramped up. He yelled out to God saying, "God, I didn't know it was going to be this painful, but I'm willing to endure it for you." I held back tears when I heard that. I forced myself to go to bed while Maurice called Hospice for advice; Hospice asked if we had received the emergency kit, which we hadn't since we just started enrollment. Hospice contacted their 24-hour doctor and asked about increasing Daniel's dosage of Oxycodone, which is all we had. Maurice had a pillow and blanket and stayed downstairs, waiting for the phone call from Hospice and he wanted to be close to Daniel in case he needed anything. Hospice told us we could increase the dose to 20mg; 45 minutes later, Daniel finally fell asleep, for the first time in a few days. He hadn't had REM sleep in quite a while. He would toss and turn in pain, sleep on the couch or while kneeling on the floor, where ever he would get comfortable for a little nap. Maurice thought that he looked comfortably asleep and saw this as an opportunity to go upstairs and get a little sleep while he could. When Maurice had come back downstairs after hearing Daniel, he discovered that Daniel had walked to the kitchen, bathroom, kitchen, dining room, living room, etc. He was all over the place and left trails everywhere he went.

July 5, I had left for work, as scheduled. I was shocked to see Daniel sitting on the couch. Before the hospital bed came in, we had Daniel propped up on the couch with pillows and blankets. This was the only way he could sleep and stay comfortable. A couple of hours after I left for work, Maurice asked Daniel if he needed to change his clothes. Maurice got Daniel's clothes and helped him stand up. Daniel put his hand on Maurice's shoulder and collapsed. Maurice has fibromyalgia, so the last 4-1/2 days took a huge tole on his legs. Maurice was squatting down while putting the pants over Daniel's feet when Daniel collapsed. He could no longer hold Daniel up by himself; Maurice began crying and said, "Daniel, I love you, but I can't do this on my own. I need you to help me." Daniel mustered up enough strength to stand, as Maurice stood and pulled up Daniel's pants. Daniel and Maurice fell into a brotherly embrace and Daniel said, "I love you too". Daniel said he wanted to be back on the couch, so Maurice wheeled him to the couch and made sure he was comfortable. Maurice turned around

DANIEL: A LIFE TRANSFORMED

to call Hospice to find out when they were planning to finish their enrollment and bring the emergency kit. While on the phone with Hospice, Maurice noticed that Daniel didn't look right. When Maurice waved his hand in front of Daniel's face and called his name, he was non-responsive; Maurice hung up with Hospice and called 911.

I received a text from Maurice at 9:43AM that Daniel was unconscious and unresponsive. I called Maurice and he informed me that paramedics were there working on him; I told him I was coming home, against his wishes. I thought I would get there, Maurice would jump in the truck, and we would head for the hospital. I arrived at the house at 10:20AM. Paramedics were standing outside, my neighbor tried to stop me as I made my way from the truck to the front door. I ignored my neighbor, and ran to the house like my life depended on it. The paramedics were in full alert thinking I would hurt myself running up all of the steps as they tried to slow me down. I asked Maurice what hospital they were taking him to. As Maurice turned to me to tell me what happened, I could see Daniel lying on the floor covered up and Maurice told me at that moment that he had passed away at 10:00 AM. I immediately started crying, called my parents, my boss, and my friend who had been worried about him. It's not easy trying to stay calm with your boss when you're fighting back tears that can't be fought back. A little later, the Chaplin came in, who happens to be a friend of mine, and I immediately ran to him and wrapped my arms around him. I was so happy to see him, like I thought he could bring my brother back to life; yes, I said brother. After all we had been through, he was more like a brother to me than anything else. He was the brother I never had and there will always be a piece missing from my heart. All of the bickering, complaining, arguing, foolishness, and annoyingness was suddenly being missed. I wanted, and needed, to hear his voice one more time. I found out a little later that his deliverance was online; I was so grateful that I got to see and hear him once more. To see the video, please visit https://www.youtube.com/watch?v=XF7eziFFNU8

God saw how much he was suffering. After what Daniel yelled out to God the night before he passed, God didn't want him going through that again. This was why God took him so quickly. It was one week short of three months from the time that he was diagnosed to the time he passed away. Daniel

DANIEL: A LIFE TRANSFORMED

always spoke of being healed with everyone. He garnered a lot of criticism for doing so, but he, and we, believed it wholeheartedly. When God told him that he was healed, he didn't mean healed in the flesh. We now know that Daniel was made whole in spirit, but his transformation of healing wasn't complete until he was taken home. He's now completely and 100% healed by God!

You see, I tell you all of this not because of the man he was, but because of the man he became. Most knew him as the man he once was… loud, obnoxious, in-your-face, a "free spirit" if you will, always wanting to have fun (any kind of fun), and certainly didn't care if you were in the middle of an important conversation with someone… he needed you to hear him immediately no matter how unimportant it was. But that's not who he was when he died. He was every bit the prodigal son. He turned from all of his evil ways to serve Jesus and was made into a person that was absolutely loving, kind, devoted, and wanted the best for everyone. When he went home, he was welcomed with open arms where God said to him "Well done, my good and faithful servant, well done."

I once read the book "90 Minutes in Heaven" by Don Piper. There's one part in the book that I wanted to convey to everyone. When we think of going to Heaven, we think that the first people to greet us are Jesus and our loved ones. Don went to Heaven after a horrible car accident took his life. Ultimately, he survived after another pastor prayed over him. My point is, Don Piper says that's not at all who greets us first. Jesus, yes obviously, but after that it's not our loved ones. The person(s) who greet us first is the person who brought us to God – they influenced us in such a way that caused us to come to God and ultimately become saved. The day I go to Heaven, Daniel will be the first person to greet me because, even though I was already saved, my relationship with God became so strong because of Daniel. I was talking with my neighbor the other day and she said he would go over there just pounding on their door… just to tell them "You'll never know what God just told me!" He influenced so many people in such a great way. So many people will see Daniel first when they reach Heaven's gate.

    He's exactly where he wanted to be – in God's arms, in no more pain, and finally with the understanding of child-like faith. My prayer for all of you is that you experience the same unbelievable faith and love that he experienced in his last days and that you all live a long, happy, and faithful life praising God.

Have you lived your life like Daniel did his? A life full of self-happiness that you've found may actually be doing you more harm than good? Do you hear God calling out to you to accept His free gift? God's gift is completely free! He doesn't ask for anything in return other than you and repentance. Jesus said in John 14:6, "I am the way, the truth, and the life. No one comes to the Father except through Me."

Matthew 10:33 says, "But whoever denies Me before me, him I will also deny before My Father who is in Heaven." Jesus said in Mark 8:34-38, "Whoever wants to be my disciple must deny themselves and take up their cross and follow me. For whoever wants to save their life will lose it, but whoever loses their life for me and for the gospel will save it. What good is it for someone to gain the whole world, yet forfeit their soul? If anyone is ashamed of me and my words in this adulterous and sinful generation, the Son of Man will be ashamed of them when he comes in his Father's glory with the holy angels."

If you feel God calling you right now and you want Him in your life and in your heart, please repeat these words:

Dear God,
I know that I am a sinner and there is nothing that I can do to save myself. I confess my complete helplessness to forgive my own sin or to work my way to heaven. At this moment I trust Christ alone as the One who bore my sin when He died on the cross. I believe that He did all that will ever be necessary for me to stand in your holy presence. I thank you that Christ was raised from the dead as a guarantee of my own resurrection. As best as I can, I now transfer my trust to Him. I am grateful that He has promised to receive me despite my many sins

and failures. Father, I take you at your word. I thank you that I can face death now that you are my Savior. Thank you for the assurance that you will walk with me through the deep valley. Thank you for hearing this prayer.
 – In Jesus' Name. Amen.

LISA CULVERWELL

DANIEL: A LIFE TRANSFORMED

LISA CULVERWELL

www.ingramcontent.com/pod-product-compliance
Lightning Source LLC
Chambersburg PA
CBHW052102110526
44591CB00013B/2321